Developing an Inclusion Policy in your Early Years Setting

by
Dr Hannah Mortimer

A QEd Publication

Published in 2006

© Hannah Mortimer

ISBN 978 1 898873 50 1

British Library Cataloguing
A catalogue record for this book is available from the British Library.

Published by QEd Publications, 39 Weeping Cross, Stafford ST17 0DG
Tel: 01785 620364
Website: www.qed.uk.com
Email: orders@qed.uk.com

Some of this material was first published as *Managing Children's Behaviour* in 2004 by Scholastic (now out of print).

Printed in the United Kingdom by Newcastle Instant Print (Stoke-on-Trent).

Contents

Introduction

The aim of the book

In one sense the actual writing of an inclusion policy is the easy part – yet it is often the part we hesitate at. Writing a policy to ensure that all children are included is one thing – it is putting it into practice and providing evidence that you do so that is the greater challenge.

This book aims to get you started with your inclusion policy and also to provide you with enough practical ideas to help with its day-to-day implementation.

This is a fascinating arena though also a daunting one for those of us who 'want to get it right', but who are concerned lest we offend or exclude in any way. This will help you think a lot more clearly about the issues. It will also help you to work together with other members of staff to develop inclusive policies such as for SEN, anti-discriminatory practice, behaviour, prevention of bullying, disability and equal opportunities. In the final chapter, there is a suggestion for bringing all of this together into one 'inclusive' Inclusion Policy.

Who the book is for

This book will be useful for early years educators working in all kinds of early years settings: non-maintained early years settings, children's centres, pre-schools, private nurseries, day nurseries, at the childminder's, crèches and schools. It will also be helpful for individuals training on NVQ courses and of interest to parents and carers of children in their early years.

Legal interpretation

This book can only provide guidance and should not be treated as an authoritative interpretation of the law, which is a matter for the courts. In other words, what we should and should not do will become clearer as cases come to court and are resolved. You will need to keep yourself up to date with current government legislation and guidance and make use of your contacts in your local authority to learn what help is available to you when putting together your own policy or interpreting a blanket policy from your employer, national organisation or the local education authority.

Chapter One

Inclusion

What is inclusion?

The word 'inclusion' has developed and widened in meaning over the past few years. There has been a movement towards better inclusion for children with disabilities and special educational needs (SEN) and also recognition that we should ensure equal opportunities for *all* the children in our care. The Early Childhood Forum is a group of early years professionals who work together for children and they have devised this very dynamic definition :

> *Inclusion is a process of identifying, understanding and breaking down barriers to participation and learning.*
>
> from *Participation and Belonging in Early Years Settings*
> (Sure Start & NCB, 2005)

When looked at in this way, you can see that inclusion in early years settings is a goal for everyone who works in the sector to aspire to. If we can also include families and the children themselves, we can make sure that all children can join in fully with the activities provided at their nursery, school, playgroup, children's centre or at their childminder's. And in the broader context, we can also make sure that early years workers feel valued and included in the work they are doing.

Members of the Early Childhood Forum have provided a helpful framework for thinking about inclusion as a process arising from a clearer strategy for action. There is a reference to their very useful pamphlet on page 54. They suggest breaking this process down into five stages:

1) **Identifying** – examining your attitudes, what you do, your policies and procedures and making sure that you are working towards inclusion of all children.

2) **Understanding** – knowing why you are doing what you are doing so that you become committed to removing barriers to inclusion.

3) **Breaking down barriers** – now that you know about and understand the barriers that exist, taking action to change resources, practice, behaviour and attitudes.

4) **Participation** – making sure that everyone, especially the children, play a part in consultation, being listened to, having their views valued, making decisions about things that affect them and joining in.

5) **Belonging** – so that each child, early years worker and family member feels and believes that they are truly accepted for themselves and treated equally.

Each and every one of us can play a role in this process and help to bring about a sea change that will embrace all aspects of our work, culture and society. The more your eyes open, the more you begin to see some of the entrenched stereotypes and value systems that people have taken for granted for years and which only serve to maintain a biased and unequal social system.

An ethos for change

Working towards an inclusion policy first involves creating the right ethos in which all children, their families and early years workers feel equally valued. You might need to set aside a regular time to consider how inclusive you are being. For example:

- Are there any community groups representing diversity or specific needs that you could usefully involve in your inclusion process?

- Does everyone in your local community understand what your admission policy is, and are there any potential barriers in terms of building, costs, cultural sensitivity and diet?

- Do families involved know what early years education you offer the children and why you do what you do?

- Are all colleagues sufficiently aware of anti-discriminatory practice and potential barriers to inclusion that they can recognise it in others and in themselves?

- Have you tried to learn about diversity and needs in a spirit of trust and acceptance and within a 'no-blame' culture?

- Is there, therefore, a non-threatening and 'safe' way for colleagues to be supported or to support each other in developing more inclusive practice?

- Do you all attend training and take time to think about issues of disability, gender, ethnicity, culture, language and religion?

- Are you becoming more confident about explaining why you do what you do with the children?

The inclusion coordinator

Usually there is one person appointed within the setting who is responsible for making sure that the inclusion policy is put into action. Sometimes separate people are responsible for race relations and equal opportunities, for SEN and for behaviour coordination. In other settings, an inclusion coordinator is responsible for all of these – this is probably the way that we will see this role developing in the future. It seems obvious to combine these areas of responsibility since, at the end of the day, each is to do with ensuring that *all* children can participate and belong.

It will be the responsibility of the inclusion coordinator to make sure that a policy is in place and that it reflects the regulations at that time: for example, anti-discriminatory regulations, SEN and disability regulations and those care standards (incorporated into the Early Years Foundation Stage framework) that relate to equal opportunities and positive behaviour management.

This policy will need to evolve in response to diversity and difference and to new regulations and guidance. For this reason, it will need to be monitored and reviewed annually with colleagues, managers, parents and carers. Sometimes this will involve gathering data and evidence (on ethnicity, gender, disability and SEN) and analysing this to identify any barriers or discrimination in terms of the curriculum, access arrangements or admissions. The inclusion coordinator needs to make sure that the policy is a working document and therefore is put into practice on a daily basis.

The inclusion coordinator will need the full support of the management, with resourcing to attend training and then to disseminate training and support to all colleagues in the setting.

Involving everyone

At the end of your 'inclusion process' you should be able to see real evidence that everyone is included and involved:

- Use your observations to make sure that each child is participating fully.

- Make sure that a full range of learning activities is available for everyone and that each child can access what is on offer.

- Personalise each child's learning so that it suits their interests, experiences and needs.

- Involve families in what the children are doing with you.

- Build on the children's particular experiences and values at home.

- Take positive action to make sure that children include each other in their play.

- Use circle time and child conferencing techniques to help the children think about fairness, valuing and respecting each other and feelings.

Getting there

Members of the Early Childhood Forum came up with this suggestion of what 'being fully accepted' means in practice:

Being fully accepted means that whatever our strengths and weaknesses, interests and inclinations, we feel we belong – in what we are doing, or not doing. Feeling able to take time out to be quiet and still feel we belong is perhaps the best measure of inclusion.

from *Participation and Belonging in Early Years Settings* (Sure Start & NCB, 2005)

Consider whether any child arriving with you tomorrow will feel welcomed and have all their needs met. Will they be able to see all aspects of their own particular life and those of others reflected in the resources, books and languages used? Will children, families and workers all feel that they belong and feel happy to be there?

Chapter Two

Legal requirements

With each new piece of legislation or guidance, there are new or revised policies that need to be in place. A chapter such as this is bound to become dated and you will need to keep yourself up to date with government and local authority guidance. For example, settings have been expected to have an equal opportunities policy in place for many years now. Though this was not actually statutory it would be looked for at inspection time and form an important part of your evidence of good practice.

Special educational needs

All maintained nursery schools, schools with nursery classes and settings in receipt of government funding for early education *must* have a written SEN policy. This policy must contain the information as set out in the conditions of grant. As with all policies, the SEN policy should be subject to a regular cycle of monitoring, evaluation and review. The requirements for the SEN policy are spelt out in the *Special Educational Needs Code of Practice* (DfES, 2001). Section 317 of the *Education Act* 1996 states that the governing body of a community, voluntary or foundation school must 'report to parents on the implementation of the school's policy for pupils with special educational needs'. This is covered in more detail in Chapter Four.

Anti-discrimination

All maintained early years provision (nursery schools, early excellence centres maintained by the local authority and children's centres) *must* have a policy under the Race Relations (Amendment) Act 2000. Nursery classes are part of the school policy also required under the same Act. Any provision that comes under social services (or the new 'Children's Services'), other than those above, by law has to have a policy under the local authority's race equality scheme. Local authorities should be requiring voluntary, independent and private settings also to have a policy on racial equality. This could be part of an integral policy for the authority though it is not actually statutory. For the purpose of this book, we will assume that it is good practice to have such a policy in place.

The picture is complex and your local authority should be in a position to advise you on this aspect of your policy making. You will also find the issues raised in Chapter 6 helpful when you start to discuss this kind of policy. Anti-sexual discrimination requirements are due in 2007, possibly at a similar level to the race relations legislation.

Disability discrimination

There is a useful document *Early years and the Disability Discrimination Act 1995: What service providers need to know* (Council for Disabled Children, Sure Start and NCB) that spells out your duties under this Act. From September 2002 this Act applied to all providers of early years services and the document suggests simple approaches that may help to ensure that disabled children are not discriminated against. As far as policy making is concerned, you do not need a separate policy on disability and access so much as to make sure that your general policies do not contravene the Act. The DDA duties apply to all early years settings: to schools and pre-schools (mainstream and special); to private, voluntary, independent and state-maintained settings; to individual childminders and to networks of accredited childminders; to education and social services (or 'children's services'). In other words, the duties apply whether or not you are in receipt of a government nursery grant. Any blanket policy that you write for inclusion must make sure that no disabled child is treated 'less favourably' and must show how you make 'reasonable adjustments' for disabled children. This is dealt with in greater detail in Chapter 5.

Behaviour policy

Each registered setting is advised to have a behaviour policy which shows how your group promotes good behaviour using positive approaches. This should be a workable and accessible document that draws together all the things that you do in your setting that encourage good behaviour in the children. It makes common sense for it to flow out of your other policies, and in particular the policies you have on SEN, anti-discrimination and on equal opportunities (more of this in Chapter 7).

Anti-bullying policy

Children cannot fully participate or belong if they are the subject of bullying and it is good practice to have in place a policy on how you define, will identify and will deal with any bullying that occurs. This is not just the province of older children and schools. Anti-discriminatory practice can grow from seeds already planted in the early years (often from other people's prejudices and beliefs) and will be reduced if we can put all our other policies that deal with anti-discrimination and meeting individual needs into practice. You will read more about this in Chapter 8 with a suggestion for how this can be incorporated into a general inclusion policy in Chapter 9.

Chapter Three

Active policy making

If your inclusion policy is to work effectively, it must be a living and breathing document. It does no good at all if, once written, it is filed proudly away pending inspection! Active policies have an inbuilt system by which they are regularly reviewed (at least annually), information is brought up to date, and there is an element of evaluation. If one person becomes the named staff member responsible for that policy, then that person can make sure that she or he keeps up to date with the subject, makes sure that the policy is implemented on a day-to-day basis, looks at the policy well ahead of the review date, reports to management on how effectively the policy has been implemented and makes sure that any updating is done at the appropriate meeting. In small settings, this is often the role of the manager or deputy manager. In larger settings, it might fall to the SEN or inclusion coordinator or named person for ensuring equal opportunities.

Blanket policies might save time but will only really be effective if they are taken apart and considered in the light of the specific setting. In this way they can become understandable, practical and workable documents. Moreover, staff members must inherently believe in them if they are to show through into daily practice. It really is useful to spend time considering your inclusion policy regularly because it helps everyone 'wear the right head' when it comes to thinking about inclusion, participation and belonging.

There is a certain thread which runs through most policies and the steps below should help you in a general way when planning any kind of inclusion policy.

Policy writing
1. *Definitions*: The policy might start with your setting's definition for whatever aspect you are writing the policy about. For example, the inclusion policy would start with a definition of what 'inclusion'

means to you and your situation that you have developed in consultation with managers, staff and parents. For example, the Early Childhood Forum agreed this definition: 'Inclusion is a process of identifying, understanding and breaking down barriers to participation and learning'. In similar vein, you would start your SEN policy with a statement about what constitutes SEN, for example: 'Any child is considered to have special educational needs if they require approaches which are additional or different to usual'.

2. *A values statement*: This section allows you to state clearly and concisely what values you hold dear. What is your vision? For example, you might want to say: 'We aim to provide a setting where each and every child feels accepted and valued. We want each child to feel happy and to grow in confidence, whatever their needs. We want all the children to develop friendly and helpful behaviour'.

3. *Who is the policy for?* You need to define who the policy is for. Presumably it will be for all staff members (including those not directly involved with educating and caring for the children), all managers or governors and all parents and carers.

4. *A description of the extent of the issue*: It is helpful to provide some overview of how wide the issue is. This could be a general statement such as you might find in a SEN policy: 'About one in five children will have additional needs at some point of their school life'. It could be a statistic collected locally and used to explain why you feel that it is important to have an anti-bullying policy, such as: 'In the local primary school, one in four pupils reported that they had been bullied at some point in the school year'. It could be a specific comment about your setting, for example: 'There are six different home languages used by children in our setting' or 'In our setting, we welcome children with a range of special educational needs including physical difficulties and developmental delay'.

5. *A commitment to action*: This would cover who would do what in what situation. For example, what will staff members and parents actually do if they feel that a child has SEN? What would happen if someone suspected that a child, family or staff member was being discriminated against? How would you make sure that the setting was accessible to all the children whatever their needs? This can either be brief, referring to the various codes in existence (for example: We identify and support children with SEN in line with the *SEN Code of Practice*) or it can spell out your system in detail. You will see an example of this starting on page 44.

6. *A whole-setting approach*: Here you can spell out that it is the duty of each and every staff member to see that the policy is put into action and not just that of the inclusion coordinator. You can also list any adaptations, approaches, resources that exist within the whole setting that will be helpful in fulfilling the policy. Perhaps you already have special changing facilities and a ramp to welcome children with reduced mobility; or you may have a staff member trained in sign language or regular input from a multilingual support worker.

7. *Awareness raising*: Here, list how you will make sure that adults and children come to understand the issues covered in your policy in ways that make participation and belonging more likely to take place. You might have thought deeply about developing your anti-discriminatory practice and be able to list courses you have been on or approaches you are using regularly. You may use 'persona dolls' (see page 34) as an aid to children's understanding of each other's points of view, cultures, beliefs and needs. You might be able to report that your setting holds a wide range of books and resources reflecting a wide mix of ethnic origin, race, level of ability and interest. You might make a point of saying how you promote positive images of disability when planning activities and selecting resources and stories.

8. *Keeping up to date*: How will you make sure that members of staff keep up to date with new guidance, legislation, publications and

training? Will one named person go on courses and disseminate information to others? What staff training do you envisage? Will the policy be updated at set intervals or whenever you have something new to add? What mechanism is in place for reviewing and updating the policy?

9. *Monitoring and evaluating the policy*: How will you actually *know* that your policy is working? What will an effective inclusion policy look like in action? How will you measure inclusion? What kind of information will you gather and how will you consult the children? How will you report back to management about the effectiveness of the policy in question?

Chapter Four

Planning your SEN policy

The SEN policy

All early years settings registered to receive Nursery Education Grant should have an SEN policy. What would an inclusive SEN policy look like? You will find a list of what should be included in your policy on the next page. The day-to-day operation of the SEN policy is the role of the SENCO.

The SENCO is also likely to lead on the writing and reviewing of the SEN policy. This need not be as daunting as it sounds because the best policies are simply maps that will help us to travel from where we are now to where we want to be. In other words, policy making should be an active and a practical process. Once you have developed an SEN policy for your setting, it is helpful to share it with any visiting professional who might be able to give you practical advice on how to make sure that your policy is inclusive. Find an opportunity to share it with parents and carers and seek their views at each stage of your policy making process.

Your setting's SEN policy needs to be brought up to date whenever there is new legislation. In any event it should also be reviewed annually, involving colleagues in discussions about how effective it has been and how well it is supporting the progress of children who have SEN. In order to provide information for your policy review, it is helpful to plan a 'practice audit' first. This means gathering information about where the service is at a particular moment. This might include asking question such as:

- Are there any children with a disability/disabilities or other SEN using the service?

- Is our environment inclusive?

- What are our strengths and weaknesses?

- What special equipment/staff/adaptations does our service have?

- Do we take into account the needs of disabled children in any changes in practice or approach as a result of new initiatives?

What the policy should contain

Your policy should contain the following information:

- It should begin with a short summary of the beliefs shared by staff regarding children who have SEN. You might, for example, say that you want all children to be entitled to a broad, balanced and purposeful Early Years Foundation Stage and that you will work with parents, carers and other agencies to achieve this. The policy should then say how you will do this.

- How will you decide which children need help and what will you do about it?

- How will you monitor, record and evaluate all children's progress and identify, assess and review any special educational needs?

- How will you provide additional resources and support for children with SEN?

- How will you publish admissions arrangements in relation to children who have SEN and how will you consider complaints about SEN provision within the setting?

- Your policy should provide information on the name of the setting's member of staff with responsibility for the day-to-day operation of the SEN policy (i.e. the SENCO).

- It should list any SEN expertise and qualifications of the staff within the setting.

- It should explain how you will all obtain training on SEN.

- What resources for supporting SEN are already available within the setting?

- Who are your local support services, and how do you access them if you need to?

You will find a suggested format on page 24 that can be shared with colleagues and used to develop or review your SEN policy.

Keeping it practical

Here are some practical ways in which you can make play and learning accessible for all children wherever possible. This is exactly the kind of information you can include in your policy.

- Try not to have 'special' activities for 'special' children or to buy plenty of 'special needs' equipment as this does not help the development of an inclusive provision.

- So often, an activity can be changed in some way rather than excluding certain children from it because they cannot 'fit in' with it. Flexible approaches and adaptable timetables and routines make this easier.

- Outdoor play areas need to contain quiet, sheltered spaces as well as busy active areas.

- Indoors, tables and equipment need to be at adjustable heights and floor spaces comfortable and safe to play on.

- Acoustics can be softened with soft surfaces, cushions, carpets and curtains, making it easier for everyone to hear clearly.

- Story times can be made more concrete by using props and visual aids.

- Communication can be enhanced by making sure that all adults are familiar with any language or communication system used by the children.

- Children can also have a communication book showing how they make their needs known.

- Make more use of colours, textures and smells to encourage different senses and to develop sensory play.

- Look for ways of making tools and equipment easy to handle by all children, such as by using foam padding wrapped around paintbrushes to make them easier to hold or non-slip mats to hold small toys into position.

- Throughout the curriculum, look out for materials, pictures and books that portray positive images of disabled people and special needs.

Monitoring and review

Your setting's SEN policy needs to be brought up to date whenever there is new legislation. This means that it will have been updated following the revised *SEN Code of Practice* in 2001 and the *Disability Rights Commission Code of Practice* in 2002. In any case it should also be reviewed annually, involving colleagues in discussions about how effective it has been and how well it is leading to the progress of children who have SEN. The day-to-day operation of the SEN policy is the role of the setting's special educational needs co-ordinator (or SENCO). It is usually helpful to use an annual parents, management or governors meeting to regularly review the SEN policy and to suggest any changes that need to be made in light of new guidance.

In order to provide information for your policy review, it is helpful to plan another 'practice audit' first. This means gathering information about where the service is at present:

- How many disabled children currently use the service?

- Have we made changes to the environment?

- What are our strengths and weaknesses now?

- What special equipment/staff/adaptations does our service now have?

- Are there recent changes in practice or new initiatives that have influenced the way we work recently?

Checklist - how good is our SEN policy?

This checklist has been adapted from the very practical book *All Together — how to provide inclusive services for young disabled children and their families* (Dickins and Denziloe, 2004).

Do the staff and management members in your setting have:

- a commitment to an equal opportunities philosophy and approach?

- a shared responsibility to address equal opportunities in a consistent manner?

Have the staff and management in your setting:

- identified any low cost changes that can be made in the next year to improve access and arrangements?

- consulted disabled users of buildings (staff/children/parents/carers) about any small changes to arrangements that might be helpful?

- ensured the display of materials that reflect a positive image of disabled people and children?

Do the staff and management in your setting:

- encourage all children to develop a positive sense of self image and a pride in their own identity?

- encourage disabled children to accept challenge and participate in a wide range of activities?

- have equally high expectations of all children and take steps to ensure that they can take sensible risks?

- know where to get guidance and support when necessary?

- have links with community professionals for direct help or training in relation to care needed by individual children?

Our SEN policy

Use this framework to develop a SEN policy for your setting (remember to consult with colleagues, parents and children).

We believe that all children have a right to . . . .

Our SEN policy aims to . . . .

Our special educational needs coordinator (SENCO) is . . . .

This is what our SENCO does . . . .

We offer admission to all children who . . . .

These members of staff have had training in SEN . . . .

We currently receive this input from outside professionals . . . .

We identify SEN by taking Early Years Action. This means . . . .

We can request further support through Early Years Action Plus. This means . . . .

We plan approaches for children with SEN in these ways . . . .

These adaptations have been made to our premises to make them more accessible . . . .

We monitor our SEN policy by . . . .

Complaints about SEN provision should be made to the SENCO initially who will . . . .

We attend SEN training regularly through . . . .

We have these resources for SEN . . . .

We keep parents and carers in touch with their child's progress through
. . . .

When a child with SEN transfers to another setting we . . . .

Chapter Five

Considering disability and access

If your setting does not already have a copy of *Early years and the Disability Discrimination Act 1995: What service providers need to know* (see page 53) then it is well worth sending for one. From September 2002 this Act applied to all providers of early years services and you need to make sure that disabled children are not discriminated against. As far as policy making is concerned, you do not need a separate policy on disability and access so much as to make sure that your general policies do not contravene this Act.

We mentioned in Chapter 1 that the DDA duties apply to *all* early years settings: to schools and pre-schools – mainstream and special; to private, voluntary, independent and state-maintained settings; to individual childminders and to networks of accredited childminders; to education and social services (or 'children's services'). In other words, the duties apply whether or not you are in receipt of government nursery grant. Any blanket policy that you write for inclusion must make sure that no disabled child is treated 'less favourably' and must show how you make 'reasonable adjustments' for disabled children. What does this mean in practice?

'Less favourable treatment'

You need to be absolutely clear that you do not treat a disabled child 'less favourably' than another for any reason related to their disability. Since there is a considerable overlap between SEN and disability, this will also include many children who have SEN (see Chapter 4). The DDA defines disability as:

> 'a physical or mental impairment which has a substantial and long-term adverse effect on a person's ability to perform normal day-to-day activities.'

'Long-term' in this sense means that the condition has lasted (or is likely to last) more than a year. Children who have been diagnosed with a mobility difficulty, significant sight or hearing impairment, learning difficulty, mental health problem, epilepsy, speech and language disorder, autistic spectrum disorder, severe asthma or AIDS might all qualify, depending on how their day-to-day lives are affected. If a child has severe behaviour problems which are related to an underlying impairment, then they too would qualify under the Act. There are two official documents that provide further information and guidance on the Act produced by the Disability Rights Commission and listed on page 53.

These are the kind of issues you will need to consider when working out how you can comply with the DDA. Very few issues are 'black and white' and may depend on test cases coming to court and receiving judgments. Nevertheless, you can be reasonably clear as to what you should do. To cover yourselves, always keep careful records of why you reached the decisions that you did and what you considered along the way. The rule of thumb is that you cannot rely on blanket policies applied to all children if they end up excluding a certain population of children. Here are some examples to give you an idea of how you need to think in order to be fully inclusive:

- You should not deny a child a place in your group if they are not toilet-trained because of an underlying condition or developmental delay. Having a blanket policy on toilet training might be problematical for you because you could end up failing to offer places to children with disabilities.

- You should not deny a child the chance of an outing or special event just because you feel he/she will not understand or benefit from it. Instead, you should plan how to make it an accessible experience for the child despite any disability.

- You cannot exclude a child with a condition such as autism because of their difficult behaviour if this was clearly related to the condition and if you did not take steps to reduce stress, manage behaviour and meet SEN.

You will find many more examples in the official guidance.

'Reasonable adjustments'

The last example above clearly requires you to make reasonable adjustments for the child's condition of autism. By getting to know the child's needs, what makes them anxious, what makes their behaviour likely to become inappropriate allows you to take steps to avoid those situations and support the child step-by-step towards more social behaviour. The first reasonable adjustment that you can make in general terms is to go through your existing policies, including your admission arrangements, and make sure that they do not discriminate against disabled children.

When you are expecting a child to join your setting, think through the session in detail and collect all the information that you will need to be able to make reasonable adjustments to your spaces, your approaches, your routines and your activities. Remember that is *you* who must make the changes, not the child.

'Welcome Profiles' can be adapted and developed in order to gather information about the child's needs on entry into the setting. These are questionnaires or structured interviews that can be used with parents or carers before a child joins you, talking about what help they require from you and what the child's own interests and views are. Open-ended questioning such as 'Tell me a favourite toy/activity/game/song . . .'; 'Is there anything that makes your child particularly frightened?'; 'How much help does she need when going to the toilet?'; or 'How does he let you know when he is cross/happy/upset?' allows you to gather honest information about all children regardless of disability. These questions do not beg a certain reply and license the respondent to describe freely the amount of help that might be needed or to celebrate a newfound independence. Take time right at the beginning of your relationship together to let parents tell their story and share their interpretation of their child.

Early Support is a government programme for providing support to young disabled children and their families. If the Early Support materials (see page 54) are used in your area, then parents will have a folder full of information that they can share with you from the start.

Access

Physical access is not one of the 'reasonable adjustments' that you have to make, but nevertheless falls within other sections of the Act. You need to consider issues of physical access, not only for any child who has disability but for their parents, carers, visitors and the professionals who work with you. You need to be thinking about:

- improvements in accessing the curriculum;

- physical improvements to increase access to buildings;

- improvements in how you provide information on disabled children in different formats.

Ofsted will be inspecting registered settings on these issues and so you should have received more detailed information from your local advisors and LEA. The Disability Rights Commission provides further information (see page 53). There is also a publication by the Department for Education and Skills (DfES) on planning duties (see page 53).

What is 'reasonable'?

The duties of Part 3 of the DDA apply to providers of services who are not constituted as schools. Therefore, all settings need to consider how they can make reasonable adjustments that include:

- the provision of auxiliary aids and services;

- making physical alterations to buildings.

However, there is also a concept of 'reasonableness' that allows you to consider what resources are available to you and what support you can obtain from outside through the SEN framework (such as through a statement of SEN) or from the local LEA, Sure Start service, area SENCO, hospital, outreach service, LEA support service or Early Years Development and Childcare Partnership (EYDCP).

'Reasonableness' takes account of a number of factors such as the costs and available resources, health and safety factors and also the interests of the other children. On the health and safety side, you should carry out a risk assessment with a view to identifying, eliminating or reducing any risk involved relating to provision for the child with disability. You would probably need local and specific advice to interpret just what your requirements might be from the same sources (above) that might provide you with outside support. The Disability Rights Commission can advise you as well.

Chapter Six

Ensuring equal opportunities

What the Law says

The *Stephen Lawrence Inquiry Report* stressed the fundamental and crucial role education has to play in eliminating racism and promoting equality of opportunity (Macpherson, 1999). There is now a wide legal framework to support this.

The *Human Rights Act 1998* conferred basic rights to all including the right to education. The *Race Relations Amendment Act 2000* introduced duties on public authorities to actively promote racial equality and good race relations. Reducing disadvantage, promoting equality and ensuring safety are also addressed in *The Children Act* (1989 and 2004), *Every Child Matters* (2003), government guidelines around inclusion and diversity, and further legislation regarding gender, sexual orientation and age.

The *Race Relations Act 1976* made it unlawful to discriminate, directly or indirectly, against a person on racial grounds. This means not discriminating on account of race, colour, nationality, citizenship, ethnicity or national origin. Included in these racial groups would be refugees and gypsy or Irish traveller families. The *Race Relations Amendment Act 2000* then enforced the additional duty on public authorities to address issues of racism and equality – to take active steps to eliminate them. Authorities are required to:

- eliminate unlawful racial discrimination;

- promote equality of opportunity;

- promote good race relations between people of different racial groups.

Racism

It is helpful for us to understand the term 'racism' if we are going to write a policy that aims to eliminate it in our settings. The *Race Relations Act 1976* defined 'racial discrimination' as:

- Direct racial discrimination – treating a person less favourably than another person, on racial grounds.

- Indirect racial discrimination – when a person is unfairly subjected to a requirement or condition that is applied equally to everyone, for example, insisting on a uniform when this would go against the religion of a certain group.

- Victimisation – victimising a person who has made, or is believed to have made, a complaint of racial discrimination.

The *Race Relations Amendment Act 2000* went further and spoke of 'institutional racism'. This is the collective failure of an organisation to provide an appropriate and professional service to people because of their colour, culture or ethnic origin. This is one of the reasons why ethnic mix on courses, in educational settings and in employment settings should be monitored. Is everyone included who would benefit and who wants to join?

Anti-discriminatory practice

Since racial discrimination can arise through deep-seated prejudices within the whole of society, many early years practitioners are now looking carefully at developing anti-discriminatory practice in their settings. This is a method of actually countering some of the myths, prejudices and generalisations that exist between different social groups. This is what anti-discriminatory practice might look like in your setting:

- Differences in identities, cultures, religions, abilities and social practices are valued and celebrated.

- All staff members recognise the impact of the social inequalities that exist in wider society and their effect on the lives of young children and their families.

- All children and adults are valued for their individuality and given a sense of belonging that promotes self-esteem. Staff respect where all the children come from and what they bring to the learning situation.

- Staff recognise and fully appreciate the importance of what is learnt and unlearnt in the early years.

If you are going to plan a curriculum of activities that is completely unbiased and accessible to all children, then you need to develop positive attitudes about providing equal opportunities and these should pervade all that you think and do at work, at home and in society. It is one thing to make sure that your activities do not allow one group of children to experience success more than any other. It is far better to actually counter anything divisive through planning anti-discriminatory practice. You will be able to support colleagues better in this area if you can share an understanding of the issues that face families in relation to gender, ethnicity, sexuality, class and disability and the impact that discrimination can have on children's chances.

Strategies that help

- Try to become aware of just how sensitive young children can be. They soon pick up messages about who is 'better' or has more power than anyone else in the setting.

- Assess what subtle messages might be expressed by your daily practice, the resources and the curriculum in your setting. Look at your books, your toys, your home corner and your activities – do they represent a wide range of diversity and present positive images?

- Make sure that your admissions policy does not (unintentionally) exclude any group.

- Try to develop non-judgmental language and respect for diversity. For example, the 'baggage' that staff members bring from their own previous experiences and attitudes can colour the way they respond to different groups within the community.

- Recognise that treating children 'the same' is not the same as treating them 'equally'. You need to recognise that the world is not a level playing field and some children will need more than usual if they are to reach their entitlements as future members of the community.

Persona dolls

Why is it that some children become targets for discrimination by other young children? It might be the fact that they dress differently or look physically different (e.g. through skin colour, weight or disability). They might come from a minority cultural, ethnic or religious group. Perhaps it is because they behave differently and this is perceived as 'abnormal' in some way, or because they do not speak the same language or find it hard to communicate with others. All children are gradually building up their self-identity and self-esteem in the early years and it is so important that they come to see themselves and their unique individuality as something positive and to be respected.

One very practical way of helping to overcome early discrimination (whether or not you have a wide diversity represented in the community you serve) is through the use of persona dolls. These are dolls (and you can make or adapt your own) to which you give a persona such as a particular ethnicity, a disability, or a certain way of life or religion.

You can give a persona doll any persona you wish in order to share information and develop values in the children. For example, you can introduce 'Mol' to the children. Mol happens to have a tiny tube in her throat which you have crafted from moulded wax (use your creativity!). Mol loves to play in the sand, the water and especially out of doors. Tell a story about all the things Mol loves to do at nursery. At some point, one of the children will notice the tiny tube. At this point, explain that when Mol was a baby, she had an illness that stopped her from swallowing properly. She saw a special doctor and she had a special operation that made it easy to swallow, but left her unable to breathe and talk properly. However, with a special tube, she can breathe and talk just like everyone else. The tube has to be kept clear and her mum and teachers help with this. This can lead into

34

a very natural conversation about Mol's needs and can serve as a useful introduction to a child with a tracheotomy joining the group or simply to widen children's understanding of different people's needs.

It is important that Mol does not join the general toy box. She has a place of honour on the shelf or table where she can be reached for from time to time to share activities with the children (such as action rhymes) or to make a particular point. Mol can have many friends. You might have Luke in his wheelchair; Mia from a new-age travelling family; Ahmed whose grandparents came to this country from Pakistan; Lara who lives with her aunt and uncle; Moses whose family attend worship at a certain temple . . . all of whom can share the story of their daily lives.

The variations are limitless and, with your own positive attitude and creativity, can fill any niche in your anti-discriminatory planning. Through the use of persona dolls, children begin to identify with others who may be 'different' in some way, and through this can develop respect and understanding. It also gives you the chance to answer some of the awkward questions that children sometimes ask in front of each other.

Remember that the children will wish to remain friends with the persona doll. The author made the mistake of getting a doll back from a group she had loaned it to, only to find the children missed her badly and invited her to join their end-of-term party!

Chapter Seven

Planning your behaviour policy

Promoting positive behaviour

Each registered setting should have a behaviour policy which shows how your group promotes good behaviour using positive approaches. This should be a workable and accessible document that draws together all the things that you do in your setting that encourage good behaviour in the children. It makes common sense for it to flow out of your other policies, and in particular the policies you have on SEN and on equal opportunities. Usually the same factors that promote inclusion, confidence and a sense of belonging also promote good behaviour. Here are some of those factors, though you will probably have more arising from your other policies.

- Encouraging all the children to feel enthusiastic in their learning.

- Making sure that all children and adults feel included in the setting.

- Findings ways of showing that you value each and every child.

- Supporting children as they arrive, depart and go between activities.

- Developing each child's sense of worth and confidence.

- Making sure that adults feel confident and develop skills for handling difficult behaviour.

- Making the transfer between settings or into school go smoothly.

- Finding ways in which each child can learn successfully.

- Teaching children to work and play within groups.

- Showing children how to listen to and communicate with each other.

- Building up children's concentration, and teaching looking and listening skills.

- Providing positive role models, especially through the adults' own behaviour.

- Making sharing enjoyable and successful.

- Findings ways of motivating each child.

- Providing nurturing and comfort where needed.

- Working in partnership with parents and carers.

- Using approaches that have been shown to support self-esteem such as circle time.

What should your behaviour policy contain?

The policy would begin with a clear set of aims followed by details of how you would achieve those aims.

The aims of the policy

Here is a list of suggestions:

- Say that you recognise and support the principles of the various codes and standards currently in place. These would include the *Care Standards Act 2000*, the *Children Act 1989*, the *Education (Amendment) Act 2000*, the *Special Educational Needs and Disability Act (SENDA) 2001*, the *SEN Code of Practice 2001* and the *Early Years Foundation Stage* guidelines.

- Comment on your learning environment. You could talk about how you provide a stimulating, calm and inclusive setting and how the staff have positive attitudes and always try to remove any barriers to learning.

- Mention how you use your resources both within the setting and beyond to help the children become active and valued members of their community.

- Mention how you ensure that staff members are kept up to date with information and approaches to help them promote appropriate behaviour and manage any difficult behaviour effectively.

- Indicate how you work towards keeping the behaviour policy up to date and how you are always aiming to improve the service you provide for encouraging positive behaviour in your setting.

How to implement the policy

Your policy should then describe how you carry out the behaviour policy in your setting. Here is a list of suggestions:

- How it is ensured that all staff understand and implement the behaviour policy.

- How staff respond to children who have emotional or behaviour difficulties.

- Any particular roles and responsibilities of staff members.

- Name the person who has special responsibility and knowledge of behaviour management issues. Usually this is the SENCO, the inclusion coordinator or the manager.

- List any special training in behaviour management that staff members have received and how you plan and monitor their training needs.

- State how you work with parents and carers to design, implement and review the policy.

You can read more this and about behaviour management in general in *Behaviour Management in the Early Years* (Mortimer, 2006)

Here is an example of a behaviour policy that could be used as a basis to design your own positive behaviour policy.

Daisychain Nursery School

Our Behaviour Policy

Our aim
- We aim to provide a setting where each and every child feels accepted and valued.
- We want each child to feel happy and to grow in confidence, whatever their needs.
- We want all the children to develop friendly and helpful behaviour.

How we do this
- We try to make each play and learning experience enjoyable and to make sure that each child can succeed.
- We use positive praise and show the children that we value what they are doing using praise, photographs and displays.
- We warn children before an activity is going to change.
- We show them how to behave in a friendly way as well as tell them.
- We sometimes work in small groups so that we can teach the children to join in and to share.
- We use a daily circle time to teach the children personal and social skills.
- The children help us to agree just a few clear rules which we encourage the children to follow with helpful reminders.
- If we need to tell a child to behave more appropriately, we do this away from an audience whenever possible.

How we respond to children who have emotional or behaviour difficulties

- If a child does not respond to our usual approaches, we talk with the group's special educational needs co-ordinator, whose name is Ella.

- She discusses the child's behaviour with parents or carers, helps us assess what the difficulties are and helps us plan our approaches.

- We design an individual behaviour plan to suit the child, based on positive approaches.

- We can call on the advice of the Behaviour Support Teacher if needed, and always notify parents or carers first.

How we involve parents and carers

- We believe that the best approaches will come if we can use the expertise of both home and setting.

- We always value what parents and carers have to tell us about their child's behaviour and can use this information to plan our approaches.

- If a child's behaviour needs an individual approach, we will discuss and share the plan with parents and carers and review it regularly with them.

These staff have had training in behaviour management and emotional difficulties: Ella S., Zach N., Sue B.

Adapted from *Managing Children's Behaviour* (Mortimer, 2004)

Chapter Eight

Anti-bullying policies

What is bullying?

If you are going to think about putting an anti-bullying policy into place, or incorporating your policy on bullying into your wider inclusion policy, then you need to be clear about what you mean by 'bullying'. If you ask older children, they are likely to tell you that bullying means fighting, using hurtful words, name calling, looking at you in scary ways, saying unpleasant things about your body shape or colour, hurting you, taking your possessions, saying disrespectful things about your family, spreading rumours about you or 'hassling' you when the teacher is not looking.

Yet we know that children in their early years are still in the process of sorting out what it means to 'be kind' and developing a respect for themselves and others – in this context, how can we regard a particular behaviour as 'bullying'? Much of what we do in early years to prevent bullying falls within the Early Years Foundation Stage (EYFS) framework – encouraging and supporting children as they progress through the learning outcomes towards the early learning goals in personal, social and emotional development.

Nevertheless, you may still come across episodes of what might reasonably be called 'bullying' and you need to have a policy in place that will define how you are going to deal with this (and be seen to be doing so). A child is bullied when he or she is exposed regularly and over time to negative actions on the part of someone else. Even if the 'someone else' is another child who did not mean it or could not help it, the effect still remains that the first child is feeling bullied and you need to do something about it. You can define bullying only by measuring the effects the acts have on the vulnerable child, and it is your duty to protect that child.

So if a behaviour is to be described as 'bullying':

- there needs to be an inappropriate behaviour on the part of one person (for whatever reason);

- the recipient needs to be 'upset' in some way;

- it needs to happen persistently over time.

Writing an anti-bullying policy

Here is a list of suggestions:

- The policy should start with your setting's definition of bullying.

- Describe how the setting and parents will decide if an incident of bullying is serious enough to warrant special steps being taken.

- A values statement – this is a clear explanation of the setting's intention to create an environment in which everyone feels safe and is safe. It sets the tone for the policy (what you believe). For example: 'Bullying is simply inappropriate behaviour that needs to change' or 'We believe that all children can get involved in bullying and need our protection'.

- Who is the policy for? You might list all staff members, members of your governing body or management committee, parents and carers and state that it is for the benefit of all the children.

- A description of the extent of the problem. If you have had real problems, then take time to study what went wrong and gather everybody's views on it. Talk to the children individually and as a group to establish how widespread the problem is. Take care to put the behaviour into the context of young children learning and developing so that young children do not become labelled as 'bullies'.

- A commitment to action – how children/staff members/parents and carers will react when they think that bullying takes place. This might involve having a named contact in the setting who parents would approach if they had concerns – perhaps the behaviour or inclusion coordinator or perhaps the child's key person in the setting. It might also involve that person sitting down with the children individually and using a no-blame, problem-solving approach to explain how each child feels and support children positively in changing their behaviour. It could involve close monitoring and emotional support for the child who is feeling upset with support for new friendships and an emphasis on making the sessions feel positive. Sometimes, you can address general issues during circle time so that all the children begin to understand codes of sociable behaviour and develop a greater respect and friendship for each other. Activities that celebrate diversity also encourage the development of mutual respect and friendship.

- Prevention – a whole-setting approach. This section can include how you will use the personal, social and emotional curricular framework and your behaviour policy to make sure that incidences of bullying are prevented.

- Awareness raising – part of preventing bullying involves carers being aware that it exists and being on the alert to the children being affected. How can parents, carers and staff be on the alert for children who might be emotionally or physically affected by the behaviour of others?

- Keeping up to date. Here, you should note down how you will keep up to date with guidance, publications and training concerning bullying. Will one person have responsibility for this? How will up-to-date information be disseminated to other members of staff?

- Monitoring and evaluating the policy. You need to write down how your policy will be monitored and reviewed. Will it be annually? Who will do it? Who will be consulted? How will they involve the children, parents and carers in this process? In other words, how will they know that their anti-bullying policy is being effective?

Chapter Nine

Bringing it all together: the inclusion policy

One way to bring together all the policies that this book has covered is to provide the bare bones of an all-inclusive 'inclusion policy'. Bearing in mind all that we have said about blanket policies and the need to tease them apart in order identify those aspects that are specifically relevant to your setting, you can use this as a starting point for designing your own inclusion policy.

Inclusion Policy

Name of setting:_____

Our inclusion policy
Inclusion is a process of identifying, understanding and breaking down barriers to participation and learning. This policy describes what we do in our setting to make sure that all children can participate, belong and develop, whatever their background or level of ability. It also describes how we aim to communicate and share with the parents and carers from our local community.

Our aims
- We aim to provide a setting where each and every child feels accepted and valued.

- We want each child to feel happy and to grow in confidence, whatever their needs.

- We want all the children to develop friendly and helpful behaviour towards each other with our positive support, encouragement and example.

Who the policy is for
This policy is for all staff members, including those not directly involved with educating and caring for the children, all managers and all those who have been vetted to work on a voluntary basis with us.

The children covered
We believe that each and every child has a right to be included. However, we also understand that certain children might need more support and encouragement than others. In particular, we are keen to provide an inclusive service for children:

- who have special educational needs or other disabilities;

- for whom English is not their first or only language;

- who belong to minority ethnic groups;

- who are vulnerable because of their behaviour or the behaviour of others (who might need our help to manage their behaviour positively or to avoid bullying from others).

In our setting, we already welcome children with a range of special educational needs including physical difficulties and developmental delay. There are several languages spoken by our families and we have families from many different faiths (here you can provide some overview of what your local issues are and how many children and families might be affected).

Our inclusion coordinator
In our setting, we have one person who makes sure that this policy is put into action on a daily basis. This person is responsible for issues such as meeting special educational needs (SEN), making sure that people with disabilities have the best access possible, ensuring equal opportunities, making sure that no-one is discriminated against, and seeing through our behaviour and anti-bullying policies. This person is called our 'inclusion coordinator'.

Name: _____

Contact details: _____

If there are any concerns or questions about any of these issues, the inclusion coordinator should be contacted first. She or he will reply to the concern within three days with a suggested action. If there are still concerns, these can be referred to our manager.

Name: _____

Contact details: _____

Meeting special educational needs and supporting children with disabilities

We identify and support children with SEN in line with the *SEN Code of Practice* and the *Disability Discrimination Act*. Any children are considered to have special educational needs if they require approaches which are additional or different to usual. We believe that all children have a right to the Early Years Foundation Stage, regardless of their ability or educational need. We also recognise the value of working alongside parents and carers and the support of outside professionals available to us.

The inclusion coordinator gets to know all children who have needs that are additional or different and acts as a first contact for parents, carers and outside professionals. The inclusion coordinator also advises staff on their approaches and interventions, though it is the responsibility of each staff member to actually meet the child's needs on a day-to-day basis.

The following members of staff have had training in SEN:

_____

_____

We identify SEN by taking 'Early Years Action'. This means that we share any initial concerns with parents and carers and plan an individual education plan together to support their child towards a few carefully chosen targets. This is followed through by all staff providing additional support and breaking activities down so that the child can benefit from them. We also believe that children have a right to enjoy each other's company and learn from each other. We try to plan activities flexibly so that all children can benefit from them. We meet every six weeks to review the plan with parents and carers and decide on next steps or whether further support is needed.

At present, we have the following resources for SEN:

_____

_____

If we need to, we can request further support through 'Early Years Action Plus'. This means that we will talk to parents and carers about involving an outside professional for further advice or assessment. We recognise that this is sometimes because *we* need that advice in order to provide the best service to the child. The aim of outside referral is to help us all understand the child's needs more fully and remove any barriers to progress.

We currently receive the following input from outside professionals:

_____

_____

We can also draw upon help from these professionals from time to time:

_____

_____

The following adaptations have been made to our premises to make them more accessible:

_____

When a child transfers to another setting or school, this is what we do:

_____

_____

Avoiding discrimination

- Each year, all staff members meet to discuss their inclusive practice, examine their own attitudes and beliefs and make sure that our practice is anti-discriminatory to all the children, families and visitors that we work with.

- We recognise that discrimination can be embedded within cultural beliefs and do our best to challenge prejudice and to provide information about our own standards within our local community.

- We make a point of listening to the wide range of views represented in our families and do our best to explain our practice clearly.

- Our setting holds a wide range of books and resources reflecting a wide mix of ethnic origin, race, level of ability and interest.

- We promote positive images of disability and diversity when planning activities and selecting resources and stories.

- We involve the children fully whenever appropriate in the decisions that affect their daily lives in our settings. We do this by tuning in to their feelings, 'listening' to their behaviour as well as their voices, offering choices and obtaining their views.

- We have attended training on the use of persona dolls and use these regularly to introduce diversity to the children.

- We collect and analyse information on ethnicity, gender, disability, special need and bullying annually so that we can continue to be aware of any issues that might affect the children's participation or the involvement of the families.

Promoting positive behaviour

- We aim to provide a setting where each and every child feels accepted and valued.

- We want each child to feel happy and to grow in confidence, whatever their needs.

- We want all the children to develop friendly and helpful behaviour and not feel bullied by others. We do this by trying to make each play and learning experience enjoyable and to make sure that each child can succeed. We use positive praise and show the children that we value what they are doing using praise, photographs and displays. We show them how to behave in a friendly way as well as tell them. We sometimes work in small groups so that we can teach the children to join in and to share. We use a daily circle time to teach the children personal and social skills. The children help us to agree just a few clear rules which we encourage the children to follow with helpful reminders. If we need to tell a child to behave more appropriately, we do this away from an audience whenever possible.

- If a child does not respond to our usual approaches, we talk with the inclusion coordinator, who discusses the child's behaviour with parents or carers, helps us assess what the difficulties are and helps us plan our approaches. We then design an individual behaviour plan to suit the child, based on positive approaches.

We can call on the advice of the following outside professionals if needed, and always notify parents or carers first:

_____

- If anyone is concerned that a child is being bullied, then this should be discussed initially with the child's key worker who will inform the inclusion coordinator and discuss with parents and carers the best way forward. We usually do this by monitoring the children closely and using natural opportunities to teach about kindness and sharing. We also use a daily circle time to encourage friendly behaviour and social skills.

- We always value what parents and carers have to tell us about their child's behaviour and can use this information to plan our approaches.

These staff members have had training in behaviour management and emotional difficulties:

_____

_____

Evaluation

We will evaluate annually how successful our inclusion policy has been by:

- monitoring the level of diversity within our setting;

- talking regularly with parents and carers and obtaining their views;

- monitoring how successfully any additional and different needs are being met;

- consulting with the children about how they feel about coming to our group;

- consulting staff on how supported and successful they feel in helping each and every child to participate.

The inclusion coordinator will report on these findings annually when the inclusion policy is due for revision.

Keeping up to date

It is the responsibility of the inclusion coordinator, with the support of the manager, to keep up to date with new guidance and legislation concerning inclusion. Each year the inclusion policy will be brought up to date in light of any changes, with a view to the children's needs and views and after consultation with staff, management committee, parents and carers.

Being fully accepted means that whatever our strengths and weaknesses, interests and inclinations, we feel we belong – in what we are doing, or not doing.

Signed: _____
Inclusion coordinator

Setting: _____

Date: _____

Copies to: staff members, management committee, parents and carers and to the following outside professionals:

_____

_____

References

DfES (2001) *The Special Educational Needs Code of Practice*. Nottingham: DfES Publications (ref. DfES 581/2001).

Children Act 1989. London: HMSO.

Children Act 2004. London: HMSO.

Disability Discrimination Act 1995. London: HMSO.

Every Child Matters: Change for Children (2004). London: HMSO.

Human Rights Act 1998. London: HMSO.

Macpherson, Sir W. (1999) *The Stephen Lawrence Inquiry Report*. London: HMSO.

Mortimer, H. (2002) *The SEN Code of Practice in Early Years Settings*. Stafford: QEd Publications.

Mortimer, H. (2006) *Behaviour Management in the Early Years*. Stafford: QEd Publications.

Race Relations Act 1976. London: HMSO.

Race Relations Amendment Act 2000. London: HMSO.

Useful books and resources

Brown B. (1998) *Unlearning Discrimination in the Early Years*. Stoke-on-Trent: Trentham Books.

Collins, M. (2001) *Circle Time for the Very Young*. Bristol: Lucky Duck Publishing.

Council for Disabled Children, Sure Start and National Children's Bureau (2003) *Early years and the Disability Discrimination Act 1995: What service providers need to know*. London: National Children's Bureau. Available from www.ncb.org.uk

Dickens, M. and Denziloe, J. (2004) *All Together: How to create inclusive services for disabled children and their families. A practical handbook for early years workers*. London: National Children's Bureau.

DfES (2002) *Accessible Schools: Planning to increase access to schools for disabled pupils*. Nottingham: DfES Publications (ref. DfES/0462/2002) Available from DfES Publications (Tel: 0845 60222 60) and the DfES website www.dfes.gov.uk/sen

Disability Rights Commission (2002) *Disability Discrimination Act 1995: Code of Practice for Schools*.

Disability Rights Commission (2002) *Code of Practice – Rights of Access: Goods, Facilities, Services and Premises*.
DRC Helpline, FREEPOST, MID02164, Stratford-upon-Avon CV37 9BR Tel: 08457 622633; www.drc-gb.org

Lane, J. (1999) *Action for Racial Equality in the Early Years: Understanding the Past, Thinking about the Present, Planning for the Future*. London: National Children's Bureau.

Lindon, J. (1998) *Equal Opportunities in Practice*. London: Hodder and Stoughton.

Persona Doll Training (2004) *Celebrating Diversity: Inclusion in practice.* Video and book available from Persona Doll Training UK, 51 Granville Road, London N12 0JH
Email: personadoll@ukgateway.net
www.persona-doll-training.org

The *Early Support Family Pack* (2004) The pack is for families with young children with additional support needs associated with disability.
The Early Support team is based at Royal National Institute for Deaf People, 19-23 Featherstone Street, London EC1Y 8SL
www.earlysupport.org.uk

Pre-school Learning Alliance (1991) *Equal chances: Eliminating discrimination and Ensuring Equality in Playgroups.* London: Pre-school Learning Alliance.
Pre-school Learning Alliance, The Fitzpatrick Building, 188 York Way, London N7 9AD
Tel: 020 76972500; www.pre-school.org.uk

Sure Start, the Early Childhood Forum and the National Children's Bureau (2005) *Participation and Belonging in Early Years Settings. Inclusion: Working towards equality.* London: National Children's Bureau.
At the time of going to press, copies of this pamphlet can be obtained from ecuadmin@ncb.org.uk

The Magination Press specialises in books that help young children deal with personal or psychological concerns. You can obtain a catalogue from The Eurospan Group, 3 Henrietta Street, Covent Garden, London WC2E 8LU.

Videos and resources on bullying from Lucky Duck Publishing, c/o SAGE Publications Ltd., 1 Oliver's Yard, 55 City Rd, London EC1Y 1SP.
www.luckyduck.co.uk